Do You Look Like Your Dog?

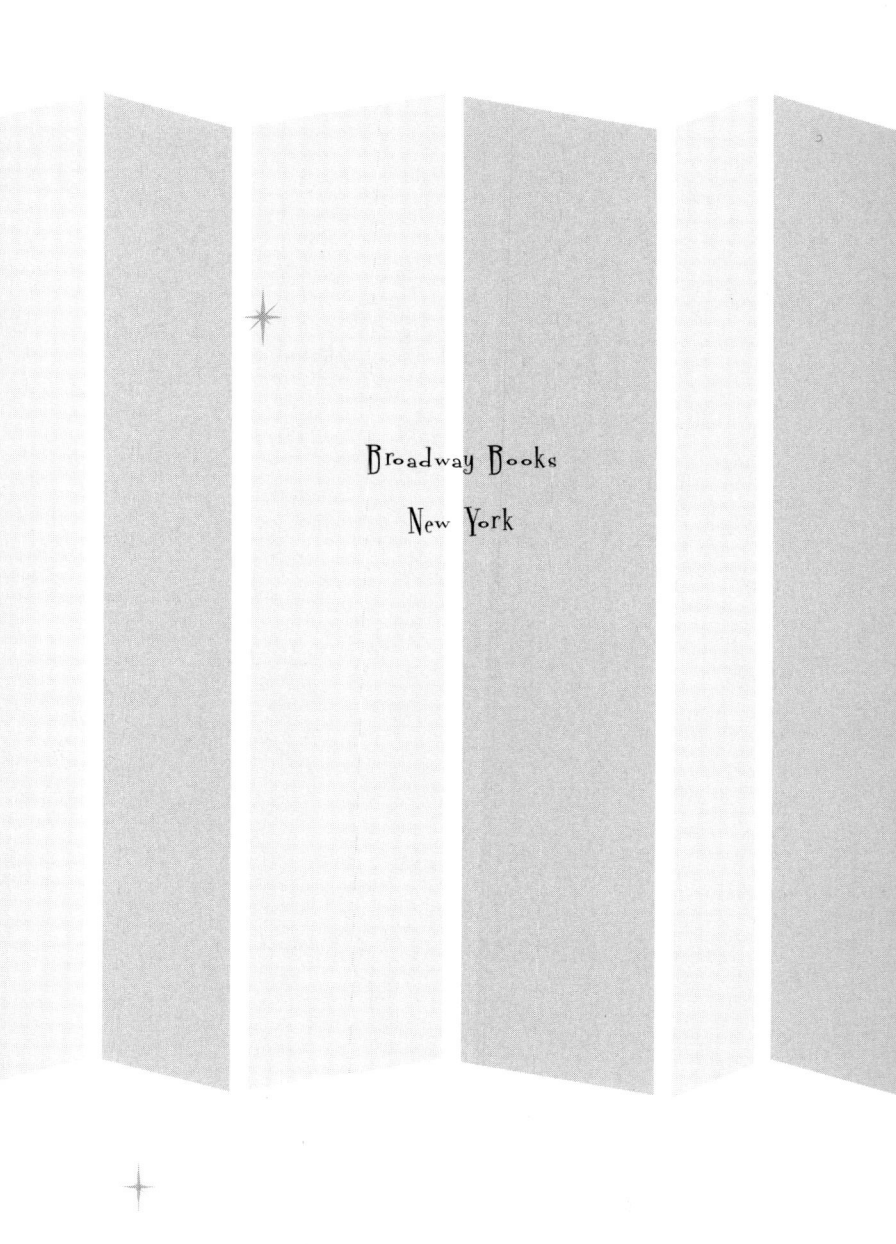

Broadway Books

New York

Do You Look Like Your Dog?

GINI GRAHAM SCOTT, PH.D.

DO YOU LOOK LIKE YOUR DOG? Copyright © 2004
by Gini Graham Scott, Ph.D.
All rights reserved. No part of this book may be
reproduced or transmitted in any form or by any means,
electronic or mechanical, including photocopying, recording,
or by any information storage and retrieval system,
without written permission from the publisher.
For information, address Broadway Books,
a division of Random House, Inc.

PRINTED IN THE UNITED STATES OF AMERICA

BROADWAY BOOKS and its logo, a letter B bisected
on the diagonal, are trademarks of Random House, Inc.

Visit our website at www.broadwaybooks.com

First edition published 2004

Book design by Caroline Cunningham

Library of Congress Cataloging-in-Publication Data

Scott, Gini Graham.
Do you look like your dog? / by Gini Graham Scott.—1st ed.
p. cm.
(alk. paper)
1. Dogs—Pictorial works. 2. Dog owners—Pictorial works.
I. Title.

SF430.S38 2004
636.7—dc22
2003058533

ISBN 0-7679-1640-9

1 3 5 7 9 10 8 6 4 2

Acknowledgments

First and foremost, I want to thank the many people who sent in their photos to the Do You Look Like Your Dog website or posed for photos at the dog shows and dog events I attended over the years. Without their contributions, this book—and the website that inspired it—would not have been possible.

Also, I wanted to extend my thanks to Peter Mason, who helped to set up the initial Do You Look Like Your Dog website about five years ago, when this book was still a proposal featuring photos from the first dog shows I attended in 1992 and 1993 at the Cow Palace near San Francisco.

Additionally, I want to thank the agent I worked with on this project, Mike Valentino, at Cambridge Literary Associates, and David Frank and Indigo Films, who are helping to turn this into a TV game and reality show, too.

Finally, my thanks to Broadway Books and Random House for believing in this project.

Gini Graham Scott, Ph.D.

Introduction

We all know or have seen someone who looks noticeably like his or her canine companion. Maybe it's a jowly guy with a Bullmastiff, a high-style woman with a clipped French Poodle, Kathy Lee Gifford and her perky Bichon Frise, Paula Abdul with her spotted Chihuahua, or Homeland Security Director Tom Ridge with his husky Yellow Labs—or even George W. Bush and his English Springer Spaniel—whatever the combination, people resembling their dogs is a phenomenon that catches our attention and amuses everyone the world over. And it has certainly fascinated, intrigued, and entertained me for quite some time.

How It All Began

About 12,000 years ago, man domesticated the dog, a direct descendant of the wolf, an animal we had already developed a relationship with through hunting. Approximately 11,988 years later, I attended my first dog show in 1992. It was the Golden Gate Kennel Club Show, held at the Cow Palace near San Francisco, and it was, and is, one of the few benched shows in the United States. A benched show is one in which people are assigned to benches by the breed they are showing, which means you get an opportunity to see people grouped by the dogs they own. Going merely for diversion, I was struck by the number of people who had a remarkable resemblance to their show-dogs. So I returned that afternoon with my camera, and I found dozens of owners who were delighted to pose and show off with their pooches—many even commented on how often they were told they looked like their dogs, or observed that many people they knew looked like their canine friends. Fittingly, the only person who didn't want to be photographed was an angry-looking woman with a scowl to match the one on her Boston Terrier—as I have learned, people often resemble their dogs in demeanor and disposition as well as in physical appearance.

Thinking the subject might make a good book, I returned to the same show the following year and took another batch of photos of willing subjects. But when other events intervened and my life got busy with consulting, teaching, and other books, I put the project on hold. As other things filled up my life, the idea languished for about six years, until one day I was working on a consulting project for a client with a Web design company. While on the project I was introduced to the client's partner, Peter Mason, and his dashing Yellow Lab. I immediately noticed the resemblance, and in the course of our conversation I mentioned the photographs I had taken; together we came up with the idea to create a website, and so www.doyoulooklikeyourdog.com was born.

Slowly but surely in the year that followed, the site began to get more and more hits. People also started sending in photographs of their own, eager to join in the fun, and to show off their resemblances to their canines. It soon became clear that the site was striking a chord with dog lovers all over the world. Though Peter had to leave the website after two years to pursue his own projects, I continued it on my own, and as word of the site spread, I began getting dozens of submissions each month—even photographs from Canada, Italy, Romania, Israel, and New Zealand. Then, about a year ago, with over five hundred great photographs, I felt ready to take the idea to a publisher, and the response was overwhelming. You hold the result of that enthusiasm in your hands.

But *Why* Do People Look Like Their Dogs?

There is no definitive answer to this question, and that makes the phenomenon both so entertaining and so interesting. There have not been any conclusive scientific studies into this common link between people and their pets, but over the years of running the website and visiting dog shows, I've come up with a few theories on why so many dog owners tend to resemble their canine companions. I've even started doing some ethnographic research, based on in-depth interviews with owners at dog shows.

First and foremost, I think there is a fairly simple psychological explanation: just as people gravitate toward other people with whom they share an affinity, so it follows that people will often choose to own pets with whom they feel some kind of connection. Sometimes the choice is very conscious and deliberate, sometimes subconscious, but often people naturally seek out pets who bear some resemblance to themselves, since physical likeness breeds a natural sense of familiarity. It's the same reason that people tend to look like their mates.

Then, too, there is the theory that people can *grow* to look like their canine pals. Just as we often observe couples growing closer in physical likeness over the years they spend together, many people will develop stronger and stronger resemblances to their pets as they live together, developing a stronger and closer relationship. This is especially true today, when people commonly think of their pets as family members. Since a person's pet is in many ways an extension of him- or herself, a dog owner's interests and lifestyle will often influence the way both the dog and owner look. For example, someone very interested in appearance might spend a lot of time grooming his or her furry friend, and both will have a similarly stylish look—many times they will have the same hairstyle, or people will dress their pets in clothes to match their own. Someone more interested in sports and the great outdoors might have a more muscular, rugged-looking pet, and that person may be more physically fit and muscular, too.

Who Looks Like Their Dog the Most, and How?

Intriguingly, certain breeds tend to look like their owners more than others. Far and away the breed with the highest incidence of resemblance in the submissions I have received is the Golden Retriever. After that, I found Collies (particularly the Rough and the Bearded breeds), Irish Wolfhounds, Lhasa Apsos, and Poodles to be breeds where people felt a great physical likeness to themselves.

It is also interesting to note the variety of ways in which people can look like their tail-wagging counterparts. One of the first things you may notice is similar hair style, length, or color, such as the women who have long flowing hair like their Collies, or the bald man who has a hairless Greyhound.

Other characteristics that owners and dogs share are facial features and expressions. A woman with a Basset Hound might have the same sad, droopy look, while a man with a Rottweiler or a Bulldog might have tough, rugged features. People will often resemble their dogs in body type, too. Often you will see a long, lean Greyhound with an owner who has a similar thin build, or a stocky and muscular man or woman with a Bullmastiff or Saint Bernard.

So, do you look like your dog? Or do you know friends, neighbors, or relatives who look like theirs? As you look at the pictures in this book, you will see that people can look like their dogs in many different ways, and there are many possible reasons why they do. But whatever the reason, it is a phenomenon that cannot be denied. Love it, laugh at it, celebrate it, marvel at it—above all, enjoy it.

How Do I Look Like Thee? Let Me Count the Ways...

It's the Hair:

The short and sheared look.

Julie David of Boca Raton, Florida, and Princess Tierra Elizabeth, a Hairless Chinese Crested.

Matching white locks.

Bruce Tripp of Oakland, California, with his Maltese, Angel.

The short . . .

Kristin Kuamstrom of Rancho Murietta, California, with Tawny Mist Secret Keeper, a Silky Terrier.

… and long of it.

Anne Ellefsen of San Jose, California, with Olav, a Bearded Collie Cross.

Big hair.

Cindy Weiner of Turlock, California, with Cody and Cruiser, her
Rough Collies. She was one of my first discoveries.

Mary Fanti of Ontario, Canada, with Sofie, her Pomeranian.

Short hair.

Suzanne McCombs of Anderson, California, with Teagan, an Irish Wolfhound.

From golden locks to silky blondes...

Jennifer Smith of Antioch, California, with Ginger,
a Golden Retriever.

Wendy McPhillips of Redwood City, California, with Lola, a Golden Retriever.

10   Do You Look Like Your Dog?

Kathy Coon of San Jose, California, with Rowdy, a Shetland Sheepdog (Sheltie). Another early find.

Shari Arata of San Jose, California, with Holly, a very Silky Terrier.

Hard to tell whether this husband and wife look more like their dogs or each other.

James Mitchell of Fair Oaks, California, with Lancelot, a Bichon Frise.

It's the Hair

Kay Mitchell with Lucky, their other Bichon Frise.

14 Do You Look Like Your Dog?

Blondes have more fun.

Sherri Regalbuto of Mission Viejo, California, with Luke,
an apricot-colored Poodle.

But brunettes don't do so badly.

Lorna Pumphrey of Stockton, California, with Kassie, an Irish Water Spaniel.

16 Do You Look Like Your Dog?

Barbara D. Beebe of Redwood City, California, with Captain and Tillie, a brace of Standard Poodles. Looks like a long, bad hair day for everyone.

Sheri Holihan of Yuba City, California,
with Chila Karis de Media Noche, a Havanese.

The ears—and hair—have it.

Terry Kelso of Novato, California, with Sadie, a Cocker Spaniel.

Hair today...

Joanne Weber of Stuart, Florida, with Daisy,
an English Springer Spaniel.

Do You Look Like Your Dog?

Rosey Gilbertson of Rochester, Minnesota, with Hawkeye,
an English Springer Spaniel.

... gone tomorrow.

Marcia O'Kane of Castro Valley, California,
with her Cocker Spaniel, Roxy.

The gang's all hair...

Linda Masys of San Diego, California,
with Muffy, a Shih Tzu.

Rachel Meyer of Santa Cruz, California,
with Journey and Sienna, Irish Setters.

Robi Anderson, a professional animal handler from Rancho Mirage, California, with Bart, a Jack Russell Terrier and an aspiring performer.

Clip job.

Clyde Schauer of Burlingame, California, with Crystal,
a Soft Coated Wheaten Terrier.

Do You Look Like Your Dog?

Double your pleasure...

Polly Armstrong of Berkeley, California, with Franklin and Theodore, two Bichon Frises.

... double your fun.

Lynne Rosebrock of Mariposa, California, with Donovan and Rosie, a couple of Irish Wolfhounds.

28 Do You Look Like Your Dog?

The next star and understudy in
AMADEUS.

Paul L. Keevil of Surrey, England, with Crosby,
a Dandie Dinmont Terrier.

It's the Hair

Bearded Wonders

Just a little off the bottom, please.

Max Spurlock of Kensington, California, with King's Mountain Westminster Abby, a Dandie Dinmont Terrier.

Sleepy time terrier.

Harold Julander of Santa Rosa, California,
with Farside, his Border Terrier.

Bearded Wonders

Peek-a-boo!

Steve Pyne of Bloomington, Illinois, with Tucker,
a Peekapoo (Pekinese-Poodle cross).

A meeting of the Executive Board.

Gary Barnett of Minden, New Hampshire, with Mae and Linny, his (sleeping) Irish Wolfhounds.

Bearded Wonders 35

Ho! Ho! Ho!

Bob Lewis of Auckland, New Zealand, with Sam,
a Poodle (Reindeer?) cross.

36 Do You Look Like Your Dog?

A set of well-clipped mustaches.

Lou Patrick of Smithtown, Pennsylvania,
with Mariah Marie, a Lhasa Apso.

Face to Face

Cheek to cheek...

Candice Morgan of San Diego, California, with Chloe,
a Yorkshire Terrier (Yorkie, for short).

Monique Groom of British Columbia, Canada, with Chatchka, a Chihuahua.

Tom Ford of Brusly, Louisiana, with Missy, his Labrador Retriever.

Susan Lane of Denver, Colorado, with Bailey Molson Riley,
a Yellow Labrador puppy.

Face-off.

Stacey Borrman of Redwood City, California,
with Candi, her Akita.

44 Do You Look Like Your Dog?

Long and lean ...

Nichole Torre of Santa Rosa, California, with Sugar Ray, her Doberman.

Jackie Lakin of Medford, Oregon,
with Sweet William, an Italian Greyhound.

Susan Sonza of Santa Rosa, California, with Anna,
a Miniature Pinscher.

All ears.

Ken Piercy of Durham, California, with Gadget, a French Bulldog.

Love that camera!

Judith Markwardt of Milwaukee, Wisconsin, with Taz, her Pomeranian.

Size Does Matter

Big guys, big dogs.

Dave Briggs of Redwood City, California, and Chris Kushner of Folsom, California, with their Bullmastiffs, Grainne and Bella, respectively.

Lance Griffin of Griffin, Georgia, with Zoe, his French Mastiff.

Size Does Matter

Big dogs, big laughs ... What's so funny?

Margo Lauritsea of Pleasanton, California, with Ripley and Molly, a pair of English Mastiffs.

In the thick of things.

Linda Hunter of Pleasanton, California,
with Willow, a Saint Bernard.

Size Does Matter   55

May to December

For some, the resemblance starts early.

Hannah Mary Cruger of Middle Island, New York,
with Benjamin, her Spaniel.

Do You Look Like Your Dog?

Brittney Bundy of Oakland, California, with Prince, her Maltese.

May to December 59

Merick Ethan Wild of Cambridge, Ohio, with Rudy, a Long Haired Miniature Dachshund.

For others, it lasts a lifetime.

Jack Taylor of San Diego, California, with Mike, a Lhasa Apso.

May to December

Tough Dogs Don't Dance

But he's really a pussycat at heart.

Clyde Shigeta of Inglewood, California, with Green, a mixed breed.

You talkin' to me?

Gene Settel of Carlisle, Pennsylvania, with Lydia, a Bullmastiff. He calls this picture "Jowls."

Whaddya bench?

Michael Wells of Montgomery Creek, California,
with Zac, a Bullmastiff.

Biker guys with biker dogs.

Mark Shaffer of San Diego, California, with Bandit, a Boston Terrier.

Tough Dogs Don't Dance

Rusty Thorsgard of Imperial Beach, California,
with T. J., his Chihuahua.

68   Do You Look Like Your Dog?

Born to be wild.

Jesse Lane of Oakland, California, and the website dogsonbikes.com, with Houdini, a Schipperke.

Tough Dogs Don't Dance

Don't Toy with Me

Girls love their toys...

April Martin of Oakley, California, with Buster Brown,
a Long Coat Chihuahua.

Carolyn Latorre of Sonora, California, with Topper, a Pomeranian.

Don't Toy with Me 73

... and so do boys!

Ray Schulte of British Columbia, Canada, with Gidget,
a.k.a. Bumblebee, a Chihuahua.

Man's Best Friend

Bobby's the one with the glasses.

Bobby Sher of Toronto, Canada, with Ricky, a Schnauzer.

God Boy Blue's the one without the glasses.

Mike McKenzie of Tacoma, Washington, with Good Boy Blue, a Catahoula Leopard Dog. He plays a mean game of Frisbee.

Man's Best Friend

Grim and grimmer.

J. Michael Bell of Lodi, California, with Street Legal, his Bullmastiff.

ME? Why don't YOU fetch for once?

Paul Keasberry of San Rafael, California, with Albert, a Rottweiler.

Man's Best Friend

Wassup?

Mike Redmon of Jefferson, Ohio, with Butch, his aptly named English Bulldog. Not only do they look alike, but they snore alike too.

A close shave.

Brad Manges of Pittsburgh, Pennsylvania, with Kenya, a Greyhound.

Mush, mush!

J. Glen Palmer of Concord, California, with Diesel,
an Alaskan Malamute.

And Woman's Best Friend, Too . . . .

Sitting pretty.

Katherine Field of New Vineyard, Maine, with Bugaboo, a Chesapeake Bay Retriever.

Things are looking up.

Dee Dee Murry of Centralia, Washington, with Hallie, her Miniature Longhaired Dachshund, both looking thoughtful.

Pugnacious?

Mary Ortez of Tracy, California, with J. J.,
the Pug with the furrowed brow.

White lightning...

Cindy Hopkins of Orangevale, California,
with Honey, a Samoyed.

Smile and Your Dog

Smiles with You

Say CHEESE!

Celia Sawyer of Torrance, California, with Aynsley, a (very) Bearded Collie.

Kathy Plante of Quebec, Canada, with
Oscar, a Labrador Retriever.

Cindy Sturges of Dayton, Nevada, with Winston, a Labrador Retriever.

Shaun Helmey of Roswell, Georgia, with Keena, his Siberian Husky.

Smile and Your Dog Smiles with You 93

Rough love.

Bonnie Kay Grindle of Santa Clara, California, hugging her one and only MacDuff, a Rough Collie.

Do You Look Like Your Dog?

White knights.

Wilna Coulter of San Carlos, California, with Whitecliff's Alexis and a Samoyed friend.

Smile and Your Dog Smiles with You

No bull!

Rob Grankni of Sunnyvale, California, with
Twister, a Bull Terrier.

96   Do You Look Like Your Dog?

Anna Virina of Ashdod, Israel, with Gosha, a mixed
breed she found on the street.

Smile and Your Dog Smiles with You

Or DON'T say cheese.

Susan Kelman of Richmond, California, with Jada, a Bulldog.

Hold that pose.

Stewart Mundy of Brentwood, California, with Jason,
a Chinese Shar-Pei.

Dressed for Success

Ready for Everest.

Jacquelyn Briley of Detroit, Michigan, with Buddy and Bamm Bamm, her two Cairn Terriers.

In the hood.

Tina Bornheimer of Newark, New York, with Kody Jacob, a Labrador Retriever. In his spare time, Kody Jacob likes to shake hands (or paws), and he also enjoys break-dancing.

Dressed for Success

Bummed out.

Lynda Long of Winnipeg, Canada, with Colby, a Border Collie/Golden Retriever mix.

Do You Look Like Your Dog?

Do you look like your dog? I do.

Sheila H. Curtis of Varnville, South Carolina, with Daisy, a Miniature Pinscher.

Dressed for Success

Checkmate.

Katie Finn of Los Angeles, California, with Gypsy,
a rescued Chihuahua mix.

Putting on the dog. Literally.

Linda Crabill of San Jose, California, with Kelly, a Lhasa Apso of international dog show acclaim.

Dressed for Success

Jackie Lockwood of Ripon, California, with Murphy,
a West Highland White Terrier.

108   Do You Look Like Your Dog?

Don Avila of Ducor, California, with Booda, his Chow Chow.

Dressed for Success 109

It's All About Knowing
How to Accessorize . . .

Great shades!

Chrystal Anne Grondin of Olathe, Kansas, with Precious Lady Princess, a very hip Golden Retriever.

Tennis, anyone?

Beth Goldstein of Laguna Beach, California, with
Laguna Mirage, an Airedale Terrier.

It's All About Knowing How to Accessorize . . .

Minnie Mouseketeers.

Joan Luna of Beavercreek, Oregon, with Scarlett, a Samoyed.

Picture perfect.

Tiffany Anne Pippin of Billings, Montana, with Bridgett, a Yorkshire Terrier.

It's All About Knowing How to Accessorize . . .

Supermodels.

Hannah Belle Crowley of Salem, Massachusetts, with George, a dashing Pomeranian.

Alexandra Blantyre of Salt Lake City, Utah,
with Shammy, a Tibetan Spaniel.

It's All About Knowing How to Accessorize . . .

SPOT the Resemblance—
101 Minus 98 Dalmatians

A great spot for sleeping.

Les and Kevin Casazza of Concord, California, taking a nap with Jewel, a Dalmatian.

Matching coats.

Teresa Utterback of Shingle Springs, California, with Domino, a Dalmatian.

Winner by a nose.

Lynn Christian of Ames, Iowa, going incognito with Agate, a Dalmatian.

Do You Look Like Your Dog?

Hail and farewell!

Michelle Rosenfeld of New York, New York, with Barbie, a Chinese Shar-Pei.

SPOT the Resemblance—101 Minus 98 Dalmatians 123

Photographic Credits

NOTE: *Except where stated below, all photos were taken by the author.*

page 2: Julie David and Princess Tierra Elizabeth, photograph by Glamour Shots
page 3: Bruce Tripp and Angel, photograph by Cleo Brown
page 5: Anne Ellefsen and Olav, photograph by Cleo Brown
page 7: Mary Fanti and Sofie, photograph by Nicole Fanti
page 12: Shari Arata and Holly, photograph by Shirley Baker
page 15: Sherri Regalbuto and Luke, photograph by Steve Regalbuto
page 20: Joanne Weber and Daisy, photograph by Cathy D. Baker
page 21: Rosey Gilbertson and Hawkeye, photograph by Proex, Apache Mall
page 22: Marcia O'Kane and Roxy, photograph by Cleo Brown
page 23: Linda Masys and Muffy, photograph by Linda Masys
page 25: Robi Anderson and Bart, photograph by Photo Galleria
page 29: Paul L. Keevil and Crosby, photograph by Tim Rose (for "Dogs Today")
page 34: Steve Pyne and Tucker, photograph by Kathleen O'Grady-Pyne
page 36: Bob Lewis and Sam, photograph by Tracy Lewis

page 37:	Lou Patrick and Mariah Marie, photograph by Michelle Patrick
page 40:	Candice Morgan and Chloe, photograph by Scott Whitney
page 41:	Monique Groom and Chatchka, photograph by Ron Groom
page 42:	Tom Ford and Missy, photograph by Kathryn Cormier
page 43:	Susan Lane and Bailey Molson Riley, photograph by Susan Lane
page 44:	Stacey Borrman and Candi, photograph by Paul Borrman
page 49:	Judith Markwardt and Taz, photograph by Expressly Photos
page 53:	Lance Griffin and Zoe, photograph by Lisa Griffin
page 58:	Hannah Mary Cruger and Benjamin, photograph by Ashley Murnyack
page 60:	Merick Ethan Wild and Rudy, photograph by Tracy H. Wild
page 61:	Jack Taylor and Mike, photograph by Pat Taylor
page 64:	Clyde Shigeta and Green, photograph by Wendy Shigeta
page 65:	Gene Settel and Lydia, photograph by Terri Settel
page 67:	Mark Shaffer and Bandit, photograph by Laura Stockham
page 68:	Rusty Thorsgard and T. J., photograph by Dayleanne Thorsgard
page 69:	Jesse Lane and Houdini, photograph by Dianne Lukash Ray
page 74:	Ray Schulte and Gidget, photograph by Mike Schwartzenburg
page 76:	Bobby Sher and Ricky, photograph by Michael Lennick
page 77:	Mike MacKenzie and Good Boy Blue, photograph by Max Ellison
page 80:	Mike Redmon and Butch, photograph by Penny Redmon
page 81:	Brad Manges and Kenya, photograph by Britta Manges
page 84:	Katherine Field and Bugaboo, photograph by Abigail R. Field
page 85:	Dee Dee Murry and Hallie, photograph by Dee Dee Murry

Photographic Credits

page 91:	Kathy Plante and Oscar, photograph by Moto Photo-Fairlawn Plaza
page 93:	Shaun Helmey and Keena, photograph by Amanda Denmark
page 97:	Anne Virina and Gosha, photograph by Victoria Komarov
page 102:	Jacquelyne Briley and Buddy and Bamm Bamm, photograph from Jacquelyne Briley, photographer unknown
page 103:	Tina Bornheimer and Kody Jacob, photograph by Janice Bornheimer
page 104:	Lynda Long and Colby, photograph by Steve Carlisle
page 105:	Sheila H. Curtis and Daisy, photograph by Charlotte Harvey
page 106:	Katie Finn and Gypsy, photograph by Gregg Edwards
page 112:	Chrystal Anne Grondin and Precious Lady Princess, photograph by John T. Grondin
page 113:	Beth Goldstein and Laguna Mirage, photograph by Patti Pracht
page 114:	Joan Luna and Scarlett, photograph by Connie Luna
page 115:	Tiffany Anne Pippin and Bridgett, photograph by Photography by Kelvin
page 116:	Hannah Belle Crowley and George, photograph from Hannah Belle Crowley, photograph by Jodi Capobianco
page 117:	Alexandra Blantyre and Shammy, photograph by Matt Paepke
page 120:	Les and Kevin Casazza and Jewel, photograph by Les Casazza
page 122:	Lynn Christian and Agate, photograph by Mike Rickard Photography
page 123:	Michelle Rosenfeld and Barbie, photograph by Herbery Rosenfeld
Cover	Jo Diliberto of Turin, Italy, with Sophia, a Chocolate Standard Poodle, photograph from Jo Diliberto, photographer unknown
Cover	Gopher Neelands of Gainesville, Florida, with Steppenwoof, a Shih-Tzu–Poodle mix, photograph by Kevin Neelands

Photographic Credits   127

About the Author

Gini Graham Scott, Ph.D., is a nationally known writer, consultant, and workshop/seminar leader who has published over thirty-five books and conducted programs on relationships, psychological profiling, and creativity among other subjects. She has won numerous awards for her photographs, many of which have previously been published in two of her books and a calendar.

Some of her recent books on relationships, psychology, and creativity include *A Survival Guide to Working with Humans*; *The Complete Idiot's Guide to Shamanism*; *Work with Me: Resolving Everyday Conflict in Your Organization*; *Making Ethical Choices: Resolving Ethical Dilemmas*; *The Empowered Mind: How to Harness the Creative Force Within You*; and *Mind Power: Picture Your Way to Success*.

She has been a guest on numerous TV and radio talk shows, including *Oprah*, *Montel Williams*, and *The O'Reilly Factor*, and her books have been featured in numerous articles and book reviews. She received a Ph.D. from the University of California in sociology; a J.D. degree from the University of San Francisco Law School; an M.A. in anthropology from California State University, Hayward; and is working on an additional M.A. in organizational/consumer/audience behavior and mass communications at Hayward.

She began developing the Do You Look Like Your Dog project in 1992 after visiting the annual Golden Gate Kennel Club Dog Show and launched the website in 1999 with the help of a client's partner, who owned a beautiful Yellow Labrador. In 2002, the website, featuring an international competition for people who looked like their dogs, began to take off, as people around the world began sending in their photos. Ironically, on her first summer job at age sixteen she worked on a children's book featuring dog stamps for Golden Books, then published by Simon and Schuster. Her job was to collect and summarize information on dog breeds. More recently, she has been giving presentations on "Why People Look Like Their Dogs," and is working with Indigo Films on developing a Do You Look Like Your Dog TV reality/game show.

To contact Gini Graham Scott about speaking, workshops, and seminars:

> Changemakers
> 6114 La Salle, #358
> Oakland, CA 94611
> (510) 339-1625
> Fax: (510) 339-1626
> Changemak@aol.com

You can visit her website at www.giniscott.com—and of course, visit www.doyoulooklikeyourdog.com.